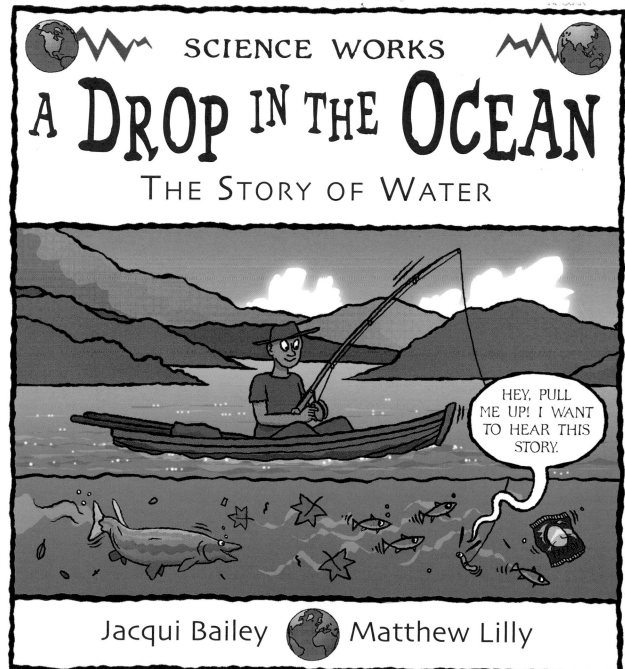

SCIENCE WORKS

A DROP IN THE OCEAN

THE STORY OF WATER

HEY, PULL ME UP! I WANT TO HEAR THIS STORY.

Jacqui Bailey ● Matthew Lilly

Picture Window Books ● Minneapolis, Minnesota

First American edition published in 2004 by
Picture Window Books
5115 Excelsior Boulevard
Suite 232
Minneapolis, MN 55416
1-877-845-8392
www.picturewindowbooks.com

First published in Great Britain by
A & C Black Publishers Limited
37 Soho Square, London W1D 3QZ
Copyright © Two's Company 2003

Printed in the United States of America.

Library of Congress Cataloging-in-Publication Data
Bailey, Jacqui.
A drop in the ocean : the story of water / written by
Jacqui Bailey ; illustrated by Matthew Lilly.— 1st American ed.
p. cm. — (Science works)
Summary: Follows the cycle of water from droplet to vapor
and back to water and its journeys in between.
Includes bibliographical references and index.
ISBN 1-4048-0566-4 (Reinforced lib. bdg.)
1. Hydrologic cycle—Juvenile literature. [1. Hydrologic cycle.
2. Water.]
I. Lilly, Matthew, ill. II. Title.
GB848 .B35 2004
551.48—dc22   2003020121

For Marie
JB

For Joanna and Raymond
ML

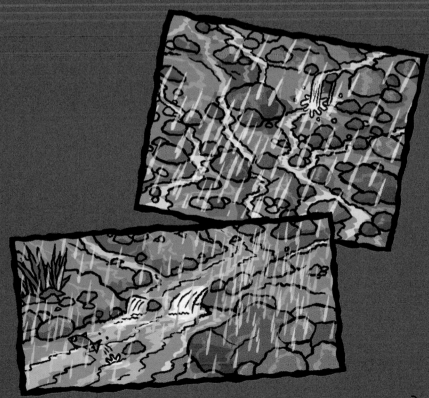

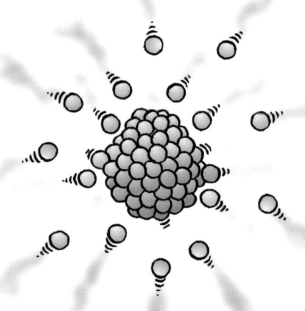

Special thanks to our advisers for their expertise:

Raymond Hozalski, Ph.D., Associate Professor of Environmental Engineering
University of Minnesota, Minneapolis, Minnesota

Susan Kesselring, M.A., Literacy Educator
Rosemount-Apple Valley-Eagan (Minnesota) School District

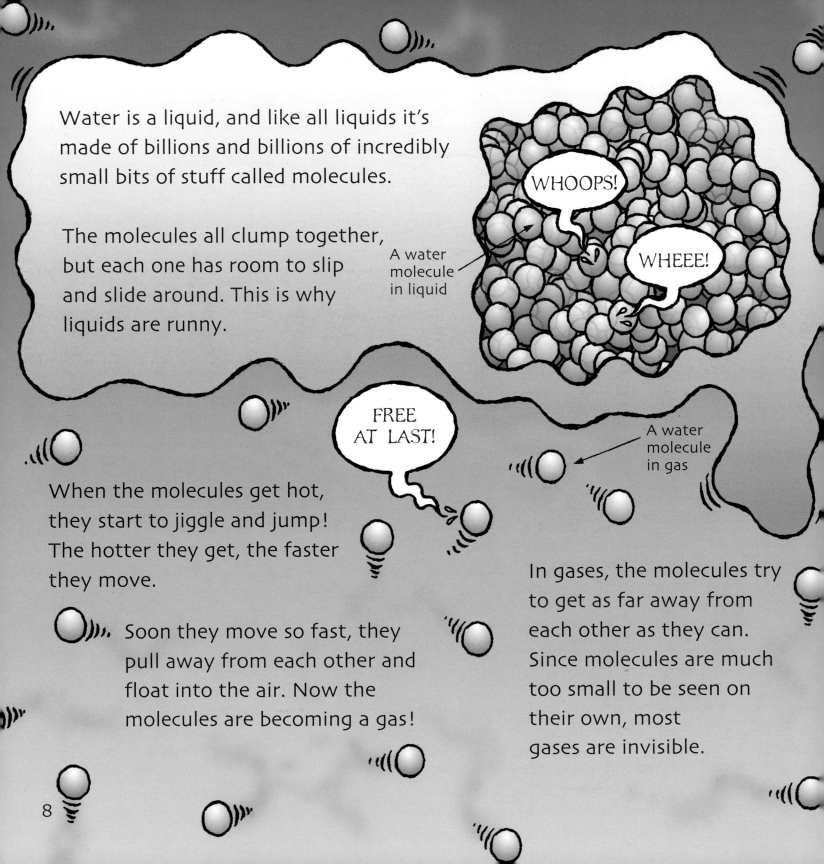

Water is a liquid, and like all liquids it's made of billions and billions of incredibly small bits of stuff called molecules.

The molecules all clump together, but each one has room to slip and slide around. This is why liquids are runny.

WHOOPS!

WHEEE!

A water molecule in liquid

When the molecules get hot, they start to jiggle and jump! The hotter they get, the faster they move.

FREE AT LAST!

A water molecule in gas

Soon they move so fast, they pull away from each other and float into the air. Now the molecules are becoming a gas!

In gases, the molecules try to get as far away from each other as they can. Since molecules are much too small to be seen on their own, most gases are invisible.

8

Back above the ocean, the water vapor drifted higher and higher into the air and spread farther and farther apart.

The molecules in the water vapor whizzed around, bumping and bouncing off specks of dust that also were floating in the air.

The higher the water vapor went, the colder the air became. The molecules got colder, too, and they started to cling to the specks of dust.

As the water vapor gathered around the specks of dust, tiny droplets formed.

The water vapor was condensing. It was changing from a gas back into a liquid.

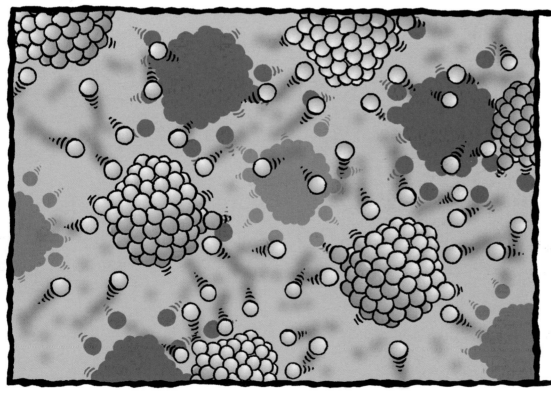

The water droplets were still very, very small, and light enough to float in the air. There were so many of them, they formed a cloud.

A cloud is just billions and billions of water droplets clumped together.

HI-HO! HI-HO! IT'S OFF TO WORK WE GO.

A breeze came along and blew the cloud toward the shore.

As the cloud traveled, it collected more water vapor. But this water vapor hadn't come from the ocean. Instead, it had evaporated from rivers, ponds, puddles, and plants.

Wait a minute— PLANTS?

11

By now, the cloud was stuffed full
of water droplets.

There were so many, they started
bumping into one another. Big droplets
crashed into smaller droplets
and swallowed them up.
The bigger droplets became so big . . .
and so heavy . . .
they started to fall!

UH-OH!
WE'RE
GETTING
HEAVY.

The droplets had grown
into raindrops.

HERE
WE
GOOOOoooo

Scientists say a droplet becomes
a raindrop when it's about as
big as this period ———▶.

Raindrops can be as big
as this circle. ———▶ ⊙
Then they usually
split in two.

13

Some of the raindrops fell on a town. They splashed onto rooftops and roads . . .

. . . slid down pipes and gutters, and trickled into storm sewers.

EEEEK!

SPLASH!

Inside the drains, the raindrops became a flowing rush of rainwater.

The sewers carried the rainwater away from the town and emptied it into a stream.

Other raindrops made puddles and pools on the ground.

HMMM ... TANGY, WITH JUST A HINT OF MUD.

HEY!

Animals came to drink from the puddles . . .

. . . and children splashed in them!

The cloud and the rain moved on. In the town, the puddles slowly disappeared. Some of the water soaked into the ground, but most of it evaporated and drifted back into the air as water vapor.

By now the cloud was floating over forests, fields, and farmlands.

Zillions of raindrops soaked into the soil. Some were sucked up by plants, but the rest traveled on . . .

SLURP! SLURP! SLURP! SLURP! SLURP!

HOORAY! A NICE COLD SHOWER.

. . . down through the soil, through the tiny spaces between the stones . . .

. . . through the cracks and crevices in the rock, until . . .

DRIP! PLIP! DRIP! PLOP!

. . . PLOP! They fell into a huge pool of underground water.

There are billions and billions of gallons of water hidden under the ground. This store of water is called groundwater, and it is made by rain.

Rain soaks down into the ground until it reaches a layer of rock or clay that's so tightly packed, the water can't get through. Then rainwater starts to fill up all the gaps and spaces in the rocks and soil above (the same way water fills up a sponge). The groundwater stays in the ground until either it seeps out into rivers and lakes, or people use it by digging wells.

Meanwhile, the cloud moved on. The wind pushed it up a mountainside.

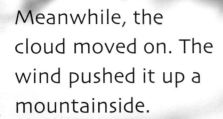

Rain poured down and trickled over rocks and stones.

The trickles became bubbling streams, and the streams joined up to make a rushing river.

YEEEE... HAAAA!

The river bounced over rocks and boulders, flung itself over the edge of a steep cliff, and crashed back to the riverbed in a waterfall.

The river became deeper and wider. Then it turned a corner and flowed into a lake.

This wasn't just any old lake, though. This lake was a reservoir—it stored water for people to drink.

But the water was too dirty to be drunk right away. It had leaves and mud in it. It had chemicals (such as the fertilizers we put on soil) and trash that people had left behind.

There were plants and fish and all sorts of small creatures in the reservoir, too, including ones we can't see, such as germs.

So first, the water had to be cleaned.

The water was pumped into a tank and mixed with a special chemical called a coagulant (co-AG-yoo-lant).

The coagulant turned into sticky blobs that sank to the bottom of the tank, taking most of the dirt with them.

Then the water went through a filter.

It slowly trickled down through a thick layer of sand until the water was crystal clear.

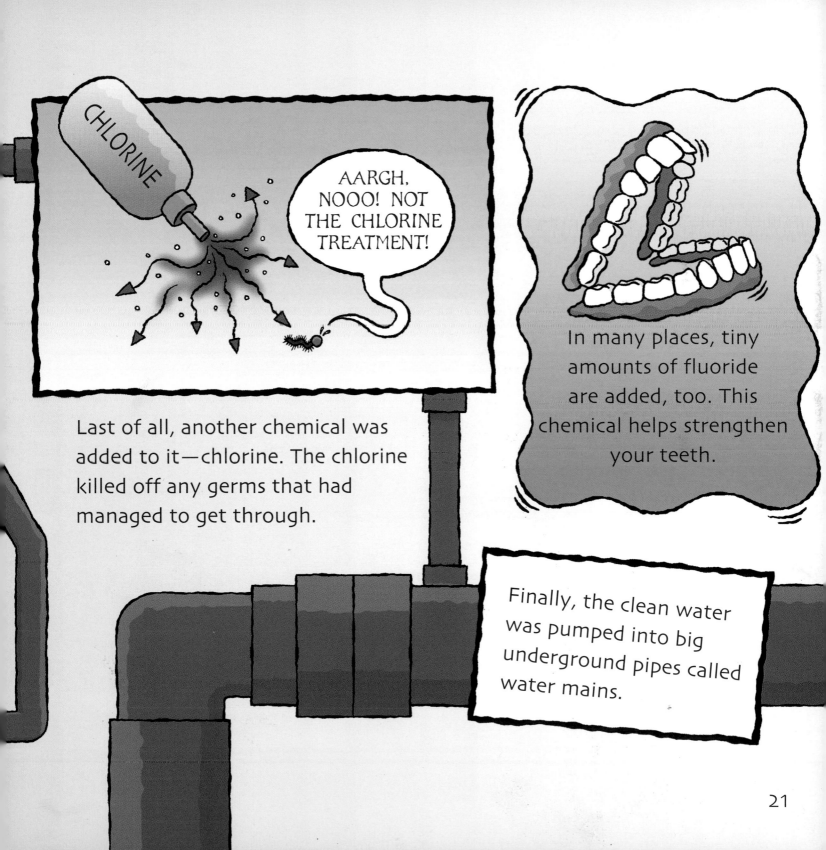

CHLORINE

AARGH, NOOO! NOT THE CHLORINE TREATMENT!

In many places, tiny amounts of fluoride are added, too. This chemical helps strengthen your teeth.

Last of all, another chemical was added to it—chlorine. The chlorine killed off any germs that had managed to get through.

Finally, the clean water was pumped into big underground pipes called water mains.

From the water mains, smaller pipes carried the clean water into offices, factories, schools, and homes. There it stayed, until someone . . .

. . . took a shower,

washed some clothes,

cleaned the car,

flushed a toilet, or

drank a glass of water.

Wastewater swirled down drains into more underground pipes called sewers.

The sewers took the wastewater away to be cleaned. This time, any solid dirt in the wastewater was settled out.

Then the water was pumped into open tanks, and air was bubbled through it to make it clean again.

At last the water was fed into a different part of the river. The river carried it back to sea . . .

. . . where it started its journey all over again.

This never-ending journey is called the water cycle. Earth's water has been traveling around and around it for millions and millions of years.

Rain falls onto the land.

The clouds collect more water vapor from rivers, lakes, ponds, and plants.

The vapor cools and condenses into water droplets and forms clouds.

Some rain falls onto soil and is used by plants.

Water vapor floats up into the air.

Water evaporates from the ocean as water vapor.

Some rain falls into streams and rivers.

Some rain sinks into the ground as groundwater and slowly seeps back into rivers and lakes.

People build reservoirs to collect some of the water. This water is cleaned and used by us. Afterward, used water is cleaned again and put back into the rivers.

Streams flow into rivers, and rivers flow back to the ocean.

And guess what? The same water that was drunk by an ancient Egyptian, or even by a dinosaur, might just have been drunk by you. Weird, but true!

25

MORE GREAT STUFF TO KNOW

Without water, life on Earth couldn't exist.
But where did all the water come from in the first place?

THE FIRST RAIN

Well, about 4 billion years ago, Earth was a raging hot ball of rocks, gases, and not much else. One of those gases was water vapor. As Earth slowly cooled down, the water vapor condensed and it began to rain.

It was the greatest rainstorm the world has ever known. When it stopped, almost three-quarters of Earth's surface was covered with oceans—just as it is today!

WATER, WATER, EVERYWHERE

Every living thing needs water, from a bug to a basketball player! Yet we never seem to use it up. Earth has the same amount of water now as it has always had.

But even though the world has lots of water, only a tiny part of it is usable by people!

About 2% of the world's water is frozen into ice (mainly at the North Pole and the South Pole).

Most of the world's water (more than 97%) is in the oceans—and it's much too salty for people to drink!

Less than 1% is in lakes and rivers, the soil, groundwater, and water vapor in the air. This is the water that humans can use most easily.

WHY THE SEA IS SALTY

Scientists think that once upon a time the oceans weren't salty at all. They think that most of the salt in the sea was dissolved from rocks.

Rainwater wears tiny pieces of rock away, and some of these rock pieces are salts. The rainwater carries these tiny bits of salt back to the sea. But when seawater evaporates, it leaves the salt behind.

Over billions of years, more and more salt built up in the oceans until the water became as salty as it is today.

THE WHITE STUFF

When air is very cold, the molecules in water vapor become tiny crystals of ice. When lots of crystals join together, they make a snowflake.

NICE PATTERN!

THANKS, I MADE IT MYSELF.

Snowflakes are no bigger than raindrops. If you look at them through a magnifying glass, you can see that every snowflake forms a perfect pattern, and every pattern is different.

Snowflakes melt very quickly on the ground, but on high mountaintops they can stay frozen for hundreds of years.

I'VE BEEN HERE AGES, YOU KNOW.

TRY IT AND SEE

THE SLUSHY STUFF

Water is magic. It can be a solid or a liquid or a gas! It all depends on how hot or cold it gets.

Try this experiment, and make yourself a treat at the same time!

You will need:
- small plastic yogurt containers
- a package of powdered drink mix
- wooden craft sticks

Following the instructions on the drink mix package, put some water and the drink mix together in a pitcher. Stir until the drink mix dissolves.

2 Pour the mixture into the yogurt containers until they are about three-quarters full. Put a stick in each container, and put the containers in a freezer. Leave them there for a few hours.

BRRR! I'M FREEZING.

What do you find when you take them out again?

The liquid has become a solid, called ice. Why? Because when water molecules get very cold, they lose energy and stop moving around. Instead, they jam themselves together in a hard lump.

3 Leave your containers out of the freezer, and you'll soon see a difference.

WHEEE! I CAN MOVE AGAIN.

The ice starts to melt back into a liquid. That's because the air in your house is warm enough to heat up the water molecules (unless you live in a fridge, that is). They're starting to slip and slide around each other again.

Let one container melt completely. (You can eat the other frozen treats while you wait!)

4 When all the ice has melted, use a felt-tip pen to mark the level of the mixture on the stick. Now put the container somewhere warm or sunny.

5 Check it every now and then during the next few days. What's happened to the water level? Where do you think the liquid went?

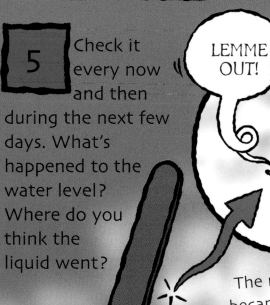

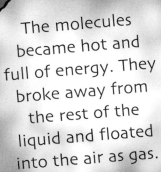

LEMME OUT!

The molecules became hot and full of energy. They broke away from the rest of the liquid and floated into the air as gas.

29

450 inches

WATERY WONDERS

The world's rainiest place is Mount Wai'ale'ale in Hawaii. On average, about 450 inches (1,143 centimeters) of rain falls there every year. It rains almost every day.

The world's driest place is the Atacama Desert in Chile in South America. It has less than ½ inch (1.25 centimeters) of rain a year. Some years it doesn't rain at all!

The Atacama does get foggy, though. And the people who live there use huge screens to condense the fog into water that they can use.

1/2 inch

Almost three-quarters of your body is made of water (about 70% of it, in fact). Even your brain is mostly made of water!

Your body loses water all the time, through sweating and going to the bathroom. You need to drink at least 6 to 8 glasses of plain water (not soft drinks) every day to replace the water you lose.

30

INDEX

FACT HOUND

Fact Hound offers a safe, fun way to find Web sites related to this book. All of the sites on Fact Hound have been researched by our staff. *http://www.facthound.com*

1. Visit the Fact Hound home page.

2. Enter a search word related to this book, or type in this special code: 1404805664.

3. Click the FETCH IT button.

   Your trusty Fact Hound will fetch the best sites for you!

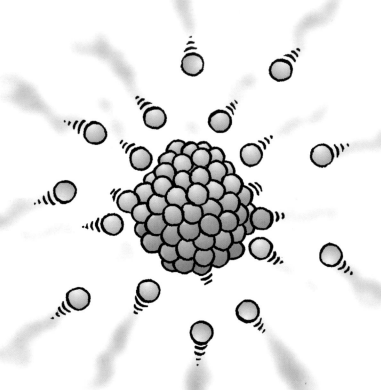